*Visiting the Past*

# The Colosseum & the Roman Forum

Martyn Whittock

Heinemann Library
Chicago, Illinois

Designed by Visual Image
Illustrations by Paul Bale
Originated by Ambassador Litho Ltd
Printed by Wing King Tong in Hong Kong/China

07 06 05 04 03
10 9 8 7 6 5 4 3 2 1

Library of Congress Cataloging-in-Publication Data

Whittock, Martyn J.
    The Colosseum & the Roman Forum / Martyn Whittock.
        p. cm. -- (Visiting the past)
Summary: Discusses the history of the Roman Forum and Colosseum, two
large meeting places, and the uses to which they were put during the
last years of the Roman Republic and the early years of the Roman
Empire.
Includes bibliographical references and index.
    ISBN 1-58810-707-8 (hard) -- ISBN 1-40340-623-5 (pbk.)
    1.  Colosseum (Rome, Italy)--Juvenile literature. 2.  Roman Forum
(Rome, Italy)--Juvenile literature. 3.  Amphitheaters--Rome--Juvenile
literature. 4.  Rome (Italy)--Buildings, structures, etc.--Juvenile
literature. 5.  Rome (Italy)--Antiquities--Juvenile literature. [1.
Colosseum (Rome, Italy) 2. Roman Forum (Rome, Italy) 3. Rome
(Italy)--Antiquities.] I. Title: Colosseum and the Roman Forum. II.
Title. III. Series.
    DG68.1 .W48 2003
    937'.6--dc21
                                    2002006326

**Acknowledgments**

For Louisa and Maria Bird, with love.

The publishers would like to thank Trevor Clifford for permission to reproduce all photographs.

Cover photograph reproduced with permission of Corbis.

Every effort has been made to contact copyright holders of any material reproduced in this book.
Any omissions will be rectified in subsequent printings if notice is given to the publishers.

Some words are shown in bold, **like this.** You can find out what they mean by looking in the glossary.

# Contents

# At the Center of the World

For more than 600 years, the Roman **Empire** grew to control land around the Mediterranean Sea, in the Middle East, and across much of western Europe. This large and powerful empire was ruled from the central city of Rome, in present-day Italy. To the people living in Rome, the city seemed to be at the center of the world. At the center of Rome itself were the Forum and the Colosseum.

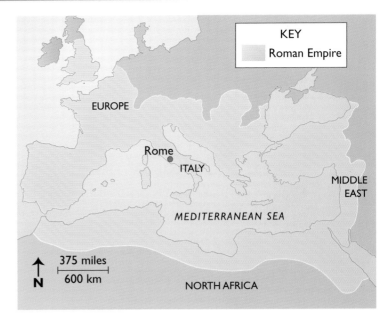

The Forum's full name was the "Forum Romanum." In the Latin language of the Romans, this meant the "Roman Forum." But what was the Forum? It was an open space used for meetings and markets, and around it were **public buildings.** These included temples, law courts, shops, and the places where the rulers of Rome met to decide how the city and the lands it controlled should be run. It was the busy, bustling, noisy, and powerful center of the growing city of Rome and its growing empire. Between the sixth century B.C.E. and 27 B.C.E., Rome was a **republic.** At that time, the Forum was a very important place.

The ruins of the Forum look like this today.

## A new center of Rome?

When Rome was a republic, it was ruled by a group of rich **citizens** called the Senate. The Senate usually met in one of the buildings around the Forum. This changed in 27 B.C.E. when a powerful Roman named Octavian made himself the first Roman **emperor.** Then only one person ruled the Roman Empire. The Senate and its meetings became less and less important, but the Forum continued to be the official center of Rome. Great religious celebrations took place there in honor of the many gods worshiped by the Romans. Victorious generals had their parades there. However, the power was now in the hands of a single emperor. The Forum was no longer the place from which the Roman world was run.

Since Roman people now had little say as to how the Empire was run, emperors needed to keep them happy. Therefore, emperors put on huge shows to entertain the people of Rome and win their support. During the shows, people fought animals, people known as "gladiators" fought other people, and criminals were executed in front of a crowd. In 80 C.E., a great new building opened near the Roman Forum. It was called the Colosseum. Thousands of people and animals died in the Colosseum to keep the people of Rome entertained. It was a new center for Rome—the largest killing place the world had seen.

The ruins of the Colosseum in Rome now look like this.

# *Out of the Marshes*

In the eighth century B.C.E., Rome was formed by uniting villages that were located on seven hills, including the Palatine and Quirinal hills. Between these hills was a marshy valley. In about 650 B.C.E., workers began to drain this wet hollow and make it a meeting place for the settlements that had united to form Rome. Around the remains of the Forum are clues that point back to the time when it was a simple marketplace where a marsh had been.

Today this area of the Forum rests on dry ground, but Romans called it the Pond of Curtius in honor of a brave citizen. A **legend** says that a chasm opened up there and would not close until a valuable possession was thrown into it. Marcus Curtius said that a brave citizen was the most valuable of all, and leapt into the hole himself.

To get rid of the water in the Forum, a great drain was built called the Cloaca Maxima. At first it was an open ditch. Later, it was roofed over and used as a **sewer** for the center of Rome. It still flows into the nearby Tiber River.

The road that ran through the newly drained marsh was called the Via Sacra in Latin. This means the "Sacred Way." It took its name from all the temples that were eventually built around the Forum. One of the earliest Roman **holy** places in the Forum was the Lacus Juturnae. This was the spring of the water goddess, Juturna, who was thought to have lived in the valley when it was a marsh.

A little shrine stood here to the goddess who was believed to look after the drain. For some reason, the Romans thought that Venus—goddess of love and beauty—guarded the **sewer.**

# Buying and Selling

The Forum was probably first used as a marketplace. On both sides of its great open space were shops called "tabernae" in Latin. On the south side were the Tabernae Veteres (the Old Shops). On the north side were the Tabernae Novae (the New Shops). These shops were often part of large buildings called basilicas. There were several basilicas around the Forum. Some of the buildings had two stories, with meeting rooms upstairs. The central place in a basilica was the nave. Law courts often met there. In the aisles around the sides of the nave there was shelter for people to discuss business and to buy and sell their goods.

The Basilica of Constantine was finished in 313 C.E. Its high arches and ceilings show how large these buildings were. In the central part were law courts. Around it were places for business.

Started by Julius Caesar in 54 B.C.E., the Basilica Julia is a good example of the way basilicas were built. The central space was the nave used for law courts. Around it was a two-story arcade containing shops. It was built on the site of the Tabernae Veteres (the Old Shops).

## Money, money, money ...

The Roman comedy writer Plautus wrote about different kinds of business done in the Forum. "In the Fish Market you will find members of dining clubs. By the Old Shops you will find the money changers. There you can borrow money." There were also bankers, barbers, and butchers. In the fifth century B.C.E., a Roman named Lucius Verginius killed his daughter with a butcher's knife in the butcher's shop in the Forum to stop her from being sold as a slave. The Emperor Caligula used to stand on the roof of the Basilica Julia and throw coins into the market below, just to watch the shoppers fighting to get them.

The Basilica Aemilia was burned down twice, once in 14 B.C.E. and again in 410 C.E. The second time it was burned by **barbarian Goth** tribesmen from eastern Europe who had captured Rome. The copper coins used by the shoppers and bankers melted into the marble floor. The green stains left by the melted coins can still be seen.

# The Center of Power

The Forum was the center of Roman government while Rome was a **republic** (509 B.C.E. to 27 C.E.). One part of it, called the Comitium, was an area where **citizens** gathered to vote on new laws suggested by **magistrates.** According to **legend,** this was where Romulus, the founder of Rome, had met the leader of the neighboring **Sabine** tribe and made peace with him. Eventually these meetings moved out of the Forum to a larger space elsewhere in Rome, where it was easier for large crowds to gather. Near the Comitium was the Rostra, a raised platform from which speeches were given.

When Julius Caesar built a new Rostra, he moved its position a short distance. He kept the curved shape at the back to remind Romans of the shape of the Comitium that had been behind the original Rostra. The slots were where the **prows** of warships, captured in battle in 338 B.C.E. against another Italian tribe, were placed as trophies. In 43 B.C.E., the head of the murdered **politician** Cicero was stuck on one of these spikes by his enemies.

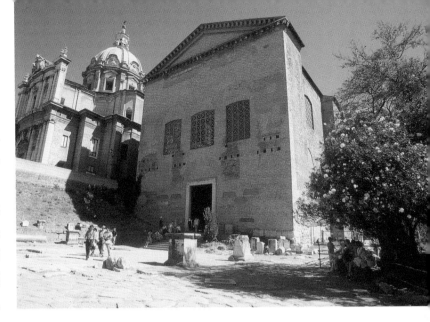

The Senate House burned down in 283 C.E. It was rebuilt but later fell into ruins after the end of the Roman **Empire**. The building there today, built in the 1930s, is a modern **reconstruction** of the original building started by Caesar and finished by Augustus.

## The Senate

The most powerful citizens of the Roman Republic met in the Senate to discuss the government business of Rome. They often met in the Temple of Castor and Pollux and made speeches from the platform in front. Powerful senators wanted people to notice them and support them against their rivals. The writer Cicero advised them: "Go down to the Forum…Be escorted by a large crowd. It brings fame and honor." In 44 B.C.E., building started on a new Senate House. This place, the Curia Julia, was where Senate meetings took place. When Rome became an empire, the Senate gradually lost power because emperors kept power for themselves. However, the Forum was still the official place from which Rome was ruled. The Emperor Galba was murdered there in 69 C.E., and in the same year the Emperor Vitellius was captured and executed in the Forum by his enemies.

Although emperors took power away from the Forum, they did not ignore this important place. In 203 C.E., Emperor Septimius Severus built this great arch covered with carvings to remind Romans of his victories in battles in the Middle East.

11

# The Homes of the Gods

**B**ecause the Forum was at the heart of Rome, many people thought that gods lived there in **holy** places. Some of these were so old that even Romans were not sure how long they had been there. There was a **sacred** fig tree with roots that were supposed to have dangled in a river there. According to **legend,** the roots caught the basket holding the babies Romulus and Remus, who were believed to have founded Rome. Near the Lacus Curtius (Pond of Curtius) were a sacred vine and an olive tree. These were so old that many Romans could not even remember why they were sacred. Near there was an altar to the god Vulcan and a statue of Romulus.

Above is the Temple of Vesta, goddess of homes. It was round like an early Roman hut. In it, six **Vestal Virgins** made sure a fire never went out. The word *Vesta* comes from a Greek word meaning "stove." The fire went out in 395 C.E. when the Christian **Emperor** Theodosius ordered the temple to be shut. As a Christian he did not believe in the **pagan** gods of Rome.

The ruins at left are of the Temple of Castor and Pollux. Only the pillars from its front survive today.

# Homes for the gods

Special buildings called temples were built as places to **sacrifice** animals to the gods. The Pontifex Maximus, the chief priest of Rome, lived in a building called the Regia. This was one of the oldest buildings in the Forum. It had been home to an early king of Rome before 509 B.C.E. Besides temples for gods such as Vulcan, Saturn, and Castor and Pollux, there were temples for leaders who were thought to have become gods when they died. It was believed that the gods Castor and Pollux watered their horses in the Forum after helping Romans win the battle of Regillus in 496 B.C.E. A temple to them was built on that site in 484 B.C.E.

Built in 29 B.C.E., the Temple of Julius Caesar treated this murdered leader as a new god. The round shape is where the altar stood, on the spot where he was **cremated** in 44 B.C.E. The altar was built outside, signifying a change in Roman worship from private to public. This change probably was to make Romans unite behind Caesar's **heir—** the first emperor, Augustus.

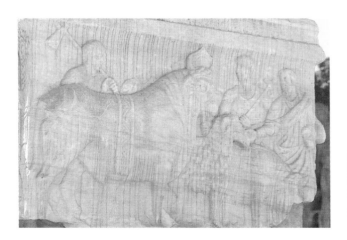

Standing beside the Via Sacra, this carving shows animals about to be sacrificed to the gods. Two men holding axes were there to kill the animals. The animals are shown draped with flowers and ribbons because they were gifts to the gods.

Sacrifices to Roman gods were made on altars such as this one.

# Justice and Punishment

Trials were held in the Forum. Some of the courts met inside the great halls of the basilicas. Inside the Basilica Julia, 180 **magistrates** worked in four law courts. Only curtains separated the different courts. Many courts were held outside in the Forum itself. Near the Lacus Curtius was a special court where non-Romans were brought to trial. This was because Roman **citizens** had more rights than non-Roman citizens and were treated differently. In all trials, 70 jurors listened to the speeches and then voted. Finally, the magistrate decided the punishments. Lawyers hired people to cheer for their side and boo the enemy.

People waiting to watch a trial inside the Basilica Julia spent time playing games on boards like this one scratched into the steps outside. People found it entertaining to watch trials. They might have been paid to cheer for one side or the other.

Law courts met in these arched rooms inside the Basilica of Constantine.

## Prison and death

Convicts were kept in a special prison near the Curia. It was built as two rooms, one on top of the other. The top room was called the Carcer. There, prisoners awaited trial. The bottom room was underground and called the Tullianum, where prisoners awaited execution. One famous prisoner kept here was the **Gaullish** leader Vercingetorix, who later was strangled. Some historians believe that another prisoner held in the Tullianum was the Christian leader Saint Peter.

Crowds watched as prisoners were thrown to their deaths from the Tarpeian Rock.

Thick stone walls kept prisoners from escaping the Carcer and Tullianum prison. There were no windows, and just one door led into the Carcer.

Only a hole through the roof allowed prisoners into the underground cell of the Tullianum. This made it impossible to escape.

# Records and Treasure

Rome was a well-educated society, and many Romans could read and write. The Forum was where they kept important written records. These records were valuable to Roman people and their government. They kept track of the decisions made by the government so people could check them later. They also contained lists of who owed taxes and who did which jobs. No well-run modern government could manage without its records. Organization was central to the Roman government.

Looking up from the Forum, any passerby would have seen the building called the Tabularium, the Roman public record office. Inside its corridors and galleries were the scrolls on which important records were kept. Important documents were also kept in the Temple of Vesta. The most famous document there was the **will** of Julius Caesar.

The Tabularium is next to the Forum on the edge of the hill called the Capitoline. It kept records of things decided in the Forum. The upper stories are not Roman. They were built in the sixteenth century C.E. by the famous Italian **sculptor** Michelangelo.

## As safe as a bank?

Some of the temples in the Forum were also used to keep valuable objects safe. The strong doors provided one defense, and many people believed that the gods would punish anyone who stole from there. In the **vaults** under the Temple of Castor and Pollux, many rich people stored their gold and silver. They could take these treasures back when they needed them. Also inside the temple were records of the weights and measures used in Rome and copies of **treaties** made by the Senate, engraved on bronze sheets. The government itself kept its treasure under the Temple of Saturn.

The thick stone walls under the Temple of Saturn made it a very safe place for the government to keep its treasures of gold and silver. Standing there today, if you look up the hill, you see the Tabularium. Just behind you is the Rostra, and a little to one side is the Curia where the Senate met during the Roman **Empire.** It was a convenient place for Rome's rulers to get to.

Important documents kept inside the Temple of Vesta (left) were thought to be protected by the fire of the goddess.

17

# The Colosseum

The huge building called the Colosseum was started by **Emperor** Vespasian in 70 C.E. His son Titus opened the building in 80 C.E. with 100 days of games. When it was completely finished in 82 C.E., it stood three stories high. Emperor Alexander Severus added a fourth floor in 230 C.E., making it about 158 feet (48 meters) high. The whole building was made to impress and entertain Roman **citizens.** Ordinary citizens had lost a lot of their power to decide how Rome was ruled after it became an **empire** in 27 B.C.E. The Forum became less important then. In a way, the Colosseum had become the new center of the Roman world.

The 80 huge entrance arches (like the one at right) held up the outer walls and allowed a crowd of 50,000 people out in just fifteen minutes. The mix of columns and arches made it very strong.

These blocks of stone (left) held strong ropes that connected to the top of the outer wall. These ropes held the edge of a large **awning** that kept the sun off people inside. Sailors from the Roman fleet worked the ropes.

18

Historians think that more than 292,000 cartloads of heavy stone blocks were used to build the Colosseum. Higher up the walls, bricks and lighter stones were used to lessen the weight being carried. The stone came from quarries near Rome.

Even after the collapse of the Roman Empire in 410 C.E., people still tried to keep the Colosseum going. This stone records how a wealthy Roman, Decius Marius Venantius Basilius, paid to rebuild it after an earthquake in 484 C.E. It seemed impossible to imagine Rome without its Colosseum.

The stone blocks just below the top of the outer wall supported masts that held up the great awning.

# *In the Arena*

The Colosseum is a large oval shape. It is 616.8 feet (188 meters) long and 511.8 feet (156 meters) wide, about as big as a modern sports stadium. Its floor was made of wooden planks, covered in fine sand brought from Egypt. The sand was there to soak up the blood of people and animals killed in the Colosseum.

## Under the killing ground

Under the floor were corridors and rooms. People and animals were kept there before they were sent up into the arena to die. The rooms are now visible because the wooden floor has rotted away.

Today the floor of the Colosseum is no longer there, so you can look down into the corridors and rooms below the arena. The pillars show where the wooden floor would have rested on them. A sandy floor would have covered the whole area in Roman times.

## A day of death

Before dawn, animals such as leopards and lions arrived for the day's events. Trained people called bestiarii got them into cages, ready for the day. At 9 A.M., the same people hunted these animals and killed them for an audience. In the middle of the morning, animals killed prisoners tied to stakes. At noon, armed men hacked down crowds of unarmed people sentenced to death. At 2 P.M., the gladiators came out. Gladiators fought each other to the death. Special workers dragged bodies out of the arena and spread sand over the blood.

These marble walls were built to keep people and animals from climbing out of the arena.

Some historians think sea battles also took place in the Colosseum, because Roman writing says that the arena was sometimes flooded. In Latin, these battles were called naumachia. These triangular drains show how water from a sea battle might have been drained from the Colosseum.

# Gladiators in the Arena

A gladiator is a person who fights other people in a bloody battle to entertain a crowd. The first gladiators were slaves who fought to the death at the funerals of wealthy Romans. They were **sacrifices** meant to please the spirits of the dead. At some point, in order to impress more people, some of these fights started to be held in the Forum. Julius Caesar held gladiator games in memory of his dead daughter. This meant he did not have to wait for a funeral to put on fights. Soon rich Romans were competing to put on the biggest number of gladiators to entertain the Roman people and win support. The first **emperor,** Augustus, put on shows involving a total of 10,000 gladiators during his 40 years as emperor.

This large gateway (above) faces west. Written evidence from Roman times tells us that the western gate was used by gladiators to enter the arena.

Opposite the great western gate is the eastern gateway. Slaves with carts dragged away the dead bodies of people and animals through it. These slaves were often dressed as Charon, Roman god of the dead.

The Colosseum had the biggest gladiator fights in the whole Roman **Empire.** In 107 C.E., Emperor Trajan had 10,000 gladiators fight there in just one set of games over a few days. Most gladiators at the Colosseum were men, but some were women. Female gladiators were finally banned in 200 C.E.

This is one of 24 small rooms that were in a narrow passageway between the arena and the first seats. Drains show that some of these were used as toilets. One wall and the roof of the passage are no longer there, so the rooms now can be seen from the arena.

Looking down through what used to be the floor of the Colosseum, it is possible to see the tiny rooms in which gladiators got ready for the fights.

# Animals in the Arena

The Colosseum was built to show the world how powerful Rome was. **Emperors** wanted to bring in animals from all over the Roman **Empire.** Besides entertaining the crowds, the range of animals showed how big and varied the empire was. They also showed that civilized Romans were the masters of the uncivilized, or natural, world of animals. The bestiarii were trained to deal with wild animals from all over the Roman Empire.

The animals included lions, leopards, elephants, crocodiles, bulls, ostriches, hippos, and deer. When the Colosseum was opened in 80 C.E., 5,000 animals were killed in the first 100 days. Many more died between then and the last animal hunt in 523 C.E.

These corridors (right) were made very narrow so that animals being driven into the arena could not turn around and bite the bestiarii.

These rooms are at the lowest level under the arena floor. This is where animals were kept.

Animals were set against other animals or against hunters called venatores. Hills were built and trees were planted in the arena to make the animal hunts look more natural. Animals were used to tear apart people sentenced to death. Prisoners were fed to wild animals as well.

## A zoo of death

In the ruins of the Colosseum, the places used to keep the thousands of animals can still be seen. Small rooms were used as cages. Narrow corridors helped keepers control the animals. Human-operated elevators carried animals up to the floor below the arena. Trap doors opened, and animals ran up ramps and out into the daylight. The animals were often frightened of the people they were supposed to kill, so their victims were splashed with blood to make the animals more savage and willing to attack. Around the arena was a platform from which archers could fire arrows to kill any animal that got out of control.

The grooves in the walls, on either side of the narrow doorway, show where an elevator pulled a cage of animals up to the arena. There were 32 of these elevators in the Colosseum. The stone in front of the doorway, with a hole in the middle, once supported a wooden post that was part of the elevator.

Looking at the Colosseum today, the ruined arches still show where tiers of seats rose high above the arena. These were the terraces where 50,000 people sat. To get so many people seated quickly, round tickets made from bone were used. The tickets showed the level and seat number, just like at a modern sports event. This made it easy to find a seat.

## Front row seats for the rich

The richest people (senators and the male members of their families) were allowed to sit on the lowest level of seats. This meant they were closest to the arena and the action. Powerful senators even had their names carved on their seats. Behind them sat wealthier Romans. Poorer Romans sat on higher levels on wooden benches. At the top level were slaves and women. The **Vestal Virgins** were the only women allowed close to the arena.

These ringside stone seats could only be used by the most powerful **citizens.** They show how close to the killing Romans wanted to be.

These under-floor corridors, called *vomitoria* in Latin, show how 50,000 people could get in or out in less than fifteen minutes. Some people think it could have been done in as little as five minutes.

This seat must have belonged to a senator because only such powerful people were allowed to have their names carved on their seats.

## No trouble on the terraces

In over 300 years of use, there is no record of a single riot in the Colosseum. Ramps and corridors under the seating levels made it easy to get in and out. This stopped people from pushing and shoving. It also meant that soldiers could get in quickly if anyone started causing trouble. Most Romans enjoyed the show too much to cause trouble.

With the fall of the Roman **Empire,** the Forum and Colosseum gradually stopped being used. The marble was taken away for use in other buildings. Cows grazed in the Forum. In the eighteenth century, the Pope stopped the destruction of the Colosseum. In the nineteenth century, excavations uncovered what had survived in the Forum.

The remains of the **Emperor's** seat show that he wanted to be very close to the action. One emperor, Commodus, who ruled from 180 to 192 C.E., even fought in the arena.

This water trough, from which people could drink, reminds us that everything was done to make the crowd's visit to the Colosseum a happy one. There were even fountains spraying perfume and fires burning **incense** to cover the smell of blood.

These carefully made brick walls, columns, and arches show how different levels of seats were raised up like those in a modern sports stadium.

# Timeline

| | |
|---|---|
| Eighth century B.C.E. | Villages on the hills beside the Tiber River begin to come together to form the town, and later city, of Rome |
| Seventh century B.C.E. | Marshy land between the hills is drained and paved to make the Forum Romanum (Roman Forum), the center of Rome |
| 497 B.C.E. | Temple of Saturn built in the Forum and later rebuilt several times |
| 484 B.C.E. | Temple of Castor and Pollux built in the Forum and later rebuilt several times |
| 338 B.C.E. | Rostra built in the Forum |
| 184 B.C.E. | Earliest basilica, the Basilica Porcia, built in the Forum by the wealthy Roman, Marcus Porcius Cato |
| 179 B.C.E. | Basilica Aemilia built in the Forum |
| 78 B.C.E. | Tabularium record house built |
| 54 B.C.E. | Julius Caesar starts the building of the Basilica Julia in the Forum |
| 44 B.C.E. | Curia Julia built in the Forum as a place for the Senate to meet |
| 29 B.C.E. | Temple of Julius Caesar built in the Forum by Augustus, the first **emperor** and Caesar's adopted **heir** |
| 64 C.E. | Saint Peter may have been kept in the Tullianum prison before his execution |
| 70 C.E. | Vespasian starts work on the Colosseum |
| 80 C.E. | Colosseum opens |
| 82 C.E. | Building work completed on the Colosseum |
| 107 C.E. | Emperor Trajan has 10,000 gladiators fight in one set of games |
| 110 C.E. | First Christian thought to have been killed in the Colosseum |
| 141 C.E. | Temple of Antoninus and his wife Faustina built in the Forum |
| 200 C.E. | Women gladiators banned from fighting in the Colosseum |
| 203 C.E. | Arch of Emperor Septimius Severus built in the Forum to celebrate his victories in the Middle East |
| 230 C.E. | Emperor Alexander Severus adds fourth story to Colosseum |
| 300 C.E. | Curia Julia rebuilt after a fire destroyed it in 283 C.E. |
| 313 C.E. | Basilica of Constantine opens in the Forum |
| 395 C.E. | The Christian Emperor Theodosius orders the Temple of Vesta shut and the Vestal fire put out |
| Late fourth century C.E. | As the Roman **Empire** declined, it became too difficult to put on expensive Colosseum games. Also, the Christian Church opposed the killing. The Colosseum declined. |
| 404 C.E. | Christian Emperor Honorius stops gladiator games |
| 410 C.E. | Rome captured by **barbarian Goths.** Basilica Aemilia burnt down. |
| 438 C.E. | Christian Emperor Valentinian bans gladiator games forever |
| 523 C.E. | Last animal hunt held in the Colosseum |

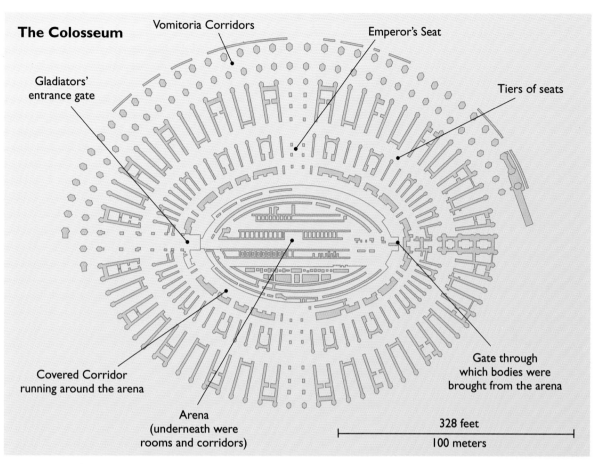

## The Colosseum

Vomitoria Corridors

Emperor's Seat

Gladiators' entrance gate

Tiers of seats

Covered Corridor running around the arena

Gate through which bodies were brought from the arena

Arena (underneath were rooms and corridors)

328 feet
100 meters

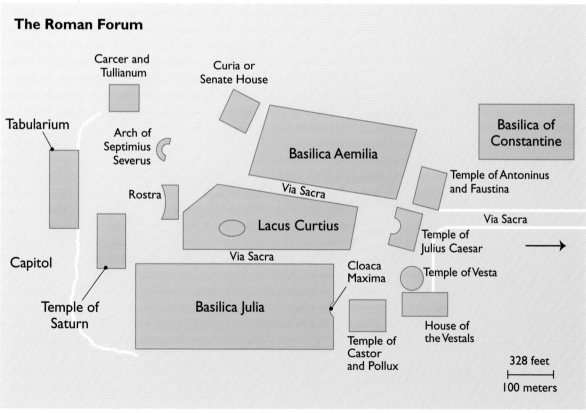

## The Roman Forum

Carcer and Tullianum

Curia or Senate House

Tabularium

Arch of Septimius Severus

Basilica Aemilia

Basilica of Constantine

Temple of Antoninus and Faustina

Rostra

Via Sacra

Via Sacra

Capitol

Lacus Curtius

Temple of Julius Caesar

Via Sacra

Temple of Saturn

Basilica Julia

Cloaca Maxima

Temple of Vesta

House of the Vestals

Temple of Castor and Pollux

328 feet
100 meters

# Glossary

**awning** cover to keep off the sun or rain. The one hoisted over the Colosseum was made of silk and hauled into place by Roman sailors.

**barbarian** word Romans used to describe people living outside their Empire

**citizen** person with rights and responsibilities in a society

**cremate** to burn a dead body to ashes

**emperor** ruler of an empire. Rome had its first emperor in 27 B.C.E., but it had been building an empire since the third century B.C.E.

**empire** collection of countries and people conquered and ruled by another country

**Gauls** tribes living in what is now France. Julius Caesar conquered them.

**Goths** Germanic people who invaded the Roman Empire

**heir** someone who receives money or power from a person who has died

**holy** something special in a religion that comes from, or is related to, a god or gods

**incense** fragrant substance that is burned, often in religious ceremonies

**legend** story passed down from long ago and believed to have some truth in it

**magistrate** person running a Roman court and deciding what sentence should be given to a guilty person

**pagan** person who worships nature or many gods

**politician** person involved in government

**prow** front of a ship. In Roman times, these often were pointed to ram and sink enemy ships.

**public building** place built by the government and used to run the city or country; can also mean a building open for people to use

**reconstruction** modern building made to look like an older one

**republic** country without a king or queen. Rome was a republic between 509 B.C.E., when Romans drove out their last king, and 27 B.C.E., when Octavian (called Augustus) became the first emperor.

**Sabine** ancient people from central Italy

**sacred** set apart as special in a religion

**sacrifice** to kill animals or people as gifts for a god or gods

**sculptor** person who carves figures or shapes out of materials such as stone

**sewer** drain that takes away waste

**treaty** agreement made between countries

**vault** space used for storage, often underground

**Vestal Virgin** priestess who tended the flame honoring Vesta in the Forum

**will** document saying who will have someone's possessions after he or she dies

# More Books to Read

Ash, Rhiannon. *Roman Colosseum.* Brookfield, Conn.: Millbrook Press, 1997.

Chrisp, Peter. *The Colosseum.* New York: Raintree Steck-Vaughn, 1997.

MacDonald, Fiona. *The Roman Colosseum.* Columbus, OH: McGraw-Hill Children's Publishing, 1996.

Mann, Elizabeth. *The Roman Colosseum: The Story of the World's Most Famous Stadium and Its Deadly Games.* New York: Mikaya Press, 1998.

# *Index*